# CONTENTS

**To my daughters Lowri and Nia**
**with gratitude for your warm support**

DANCE WITH

by

Barbara Daniels



Fareham, Hants PO16 7AL
(Tel 01329 822530)

Sponsored by Rosemary Arthur

Photograph of author by Huw Thomas, Newport, Pembrokeshire.

Edited by Johnathon Clifford 8/3/99

Poems previously published in *Acumen, Aireings, Apostrophe, Candelabrum, Envoi, Frogmore Papers, Iota, Krax, Literary Review, London Magazine, Poetry Nottingham International, Purple Patch, Seam, Slipstream, Staple, T.O.P.S., Various Artists* and *Yellow Crane*. Barbara Daniels has also won, or been commended in, a wide variety of poetry competitions, including First Prize in the Ledbury Poetry Festival Competition.



ISBN 1 900726 76 9

## DON'T TAKE IT HOME WITH YOU

In films, after a shoot-out, someone chalks
an outline of the corpse flopped on the set;
the cadaver, failed actor, wounded, forks
his legs and forms a pin-man silhouette.

He knew it was a walk-on part but thought
he'd make his mark in other ways than this:
walk on, drop dead - no matter how he fought
Clint Eastwood always won and got the kiss.

"How was your day?" his wife asks. He replies:
"As usual. That's life. I can't complain."
Inside his hollow contour something dies,
bleeds a few minutes, then gets up again.

# TO THE MUSIC OF TIME

Dance with me, woman: in your womb
I feed on heart-beats, withhold love
until you birth me: mangering, move,
fluid, the One, in my practice room.
        Dance with me

teacher, preacher, through paper worlds,
lightened with blank sheets, I will lead,
side-step, trip easy - your brain bleeds -
tap-shoes mimic the shock of words.
        Dance with me

lover, partner: my fastened veils,
testing, requesting: will you do?
I'll tango with intent, renew
palpation with bright fingernails.
        Dance with me

husband, chosen: reserve this waltz,
hold me, lids down, fecund, be slow,
man that my waiting teemings know
will seed me, serve me: true, true, false?
        Dance with me

reader, consumer, guess the score,
how do my footfalls suit your feet?
Check in, check out, come forth, retreat,
choreographer: here's client, whore.
        Dance with me

Elde[1], dread age, a mute gavotte,
deafened by endings, sack the band,
beg silence glue our folded hands -
enter the soloist I forgot:
        dance with me

death, faithful, who crossed on my card,
before my soft shoes knew the floor,
black evening tails now, evermore,
dance with me, old friend, dance me hard.

[1] *Elde: A medieval allegorical figure representing old age.*

## PLAYING THE PART

Tonight, tomorrow, I must play Macbeth,
I know the lines, I know the man - his mind
is sealed on mine: musing, dreaming I find
his thoughts and motions natural as breath.

More than my own words, his are in my heart,
learned and rehearsed and etched along my nerves,
they redirect my harmless hand - it swerves
to seize the guilt I need to take his part.

Suspending judgement, I become the one
who kills a king, a friend, a family,
these massacres, performed with empathy
engrave me with the evil he has done.

The life I once called real seems flimsy now,
extemporary, make-shift, improvised;
but butchery, ambition - memorised -
are goals that I no longer disallow.

This role is mine: the place where once I stood
is far behind; like him I wade in blood
with no return. I would not if I could
shrink from the lights to my obscure selfhood.
I wait at Dunsinane for Birnam Wood.

ELECTRICAL IMPULSES
(*in the heart, when irregular, are a sign of normality*)

In bed, embedded, stethoscoped,
so one heart caught the other's race,
out-rivalling your random pace,
I beating wildly, wildly hoped

that you, like me, could not return
to even flow, but now I learn

that hearts take chaos as their norm.
I was deceived by turbulence,
electrified by violence,
to find it signalled calm, not storm.

## THE UNRELIABLE NATURE OF DIALOGUE

I) "I love you, too": his metred words confirm
the motive for the ravelled sheets, messed bed -
these surely start with passion, not with sperm's
desire to rest its speculating head.
She wears a baby smile, looks for return,
discomfited, examines what he said.

Who made the phone call; rearranged her time;
drew curtains; set the table; cleared a space
within her mind for listening; took the wine
he'd bought - just now - with gratitude; displaced
preferences, instincts, quirks; made anodyne
her conversation, bathroom, food and face?

And who now notices that 'I love you',
invested (now the dividend is due)
may bear an added premium of 'too'?

II) A crisis, writer's crossroad: "I don't know
why I can't - won't - join other modes I've found:
the inchoate, the ragged raw, the slow . . ."
He says: "Have you read any Ezra Pound?"

A little - not enough. He fills the gaps.
At length I'm quite conversant, listening hard,
we're still in bed, my hand strays . . . perhaps . . .
He's into Leibniz, monads - I discard

something, not yet defined, within. He'll prove
his words material and relevant,
and so they are — and yet they are not love.
Tonight, I'll silently mug up on Kant.

III) "How do I look?" I shimmy. "You look just fine."
"You're sure? This dress . . . is it . . .?" "Just fine." He nods
and quickly rises (from his chair!) in time
to catch the phone on its first ring. What odds

would you lay that his hand would have grabbed me?
"I can't talk now," his voice is thick, "we're just
going . . ." ". . . to bed . . ." I pitch it so that she (?)
can hear. He carries on: "Yes, yes, we must . . ."

The receiver's hooked again. His smile's too bright.
That tricksy 'just' tickles me with mistrust.
"Hurry, my love," he pats me, out of sight,
"dinner's on me tonight. It's only just."

IV) This all-attentive she, (or is it I?)
is satisfied, almost. With every glass
she's sparkled and he's charmed: they clarify
their intercourse. In vino, veritas
slips through - she hopes. He even meets her eye
and, miracle, his hand greets hers just as

hers slides across the table, "Now," says he,
"do you believe me, now, that I love you,
your mind as well as body. Listen to me:
you share my interests, I know you love me too . . ."
(she marks the 'too', its reciprocity)
" . . . those accusations, now, they're just not true."

She tries to overlook that 'just', but how
some nibbling words can undercut his vow:
this time her mental tape records the 'now.'

## PROJECTION

Back there when I was certain that the waiting world was round,
I believed that life was geometry, that solutions could be found,
I calculated angles, I measured lines and curves,
for careful computation gets the answer it deserves.

But knowing you and loving you has disarranged all that,
the globe I neatly rationalised has edges and lies flat,
and I have fallen off it to another universe
that no theorem that I have proved can help me to traverse.

I have learned to live with mystery, I no longer look for land,
in a space composed of tangents and no compass in my hand.
The formula that rules me now I do not understand.

# NEO-DARWINISM

The fig, to replicate its genes,
has recourse to such complex means,
it strains the scientific mind
to explain what the lenses find.
The genus *Ficus* is quite big:
there are nine hundred kinds of fig;
each needs a special wasp or fly
of family *Agaonidae*,
and, with this microscopic creature,
has formed a system whose main feature
is symbiotic tit-for tat.
I'm boring you?

                    I'll stop at that
and pause while each of us reflects
on why mankind developed sex.
The fig, in Evolutionspeak,
could be considered Nature's peak:
compared to this our method's crude,
indelicate and rather rude.
We tacitly define its status
by covering our apparatus,
and, as a symbol of our shame,
it even lacks a decent name.

Yet, if I could I would not cleanse
this blot from *Homo sapiens*:
the fig's a miracle, that's true,
but so are love - and lust - and you.

# TWELFTH NIGHT

The official end of tinsel: take it down,
bin-bag that desiccated holly wreath,
Hoover the stabbing pine-needles beneath
the tree. Forget the red and green. Now brown

spreads through the house. Lords of misrule, deposed,
leave space where order reinstates itself,
baubles that danced are wallflowers - on the shelf -
routine invites no partners. We have closed

the spangled box and tidied toys away.
I straighten up. Relief. To work. Enough
of easy meats. Let's bite on something tough,
tear wrappings off an ordinary day.

## CHANGE OF ADDRESS

I've paid my taxes, postponed death, but now,
the third great certainty: I'm moving
house - all week I'm packing, cramming, shoving
shoes, mugs, coat-hangers, onions . . . onions? Now

too soon, the van is here. Three urgent men
jump out, leap in, glower round, complain; I'm standing
cradling my cringing spider-plant; they're handling
tea-chests, black bags, a mattress, mirror, when

I, drowning in possessions, note my little
life, slovenly, redundant, like the fluff
in bedroom corners, betrayed behind the stuff
I've anchored and they're shifting. "Mind out, it'll

knock that picture off!". . . that's me with roses,
forgotten, still in place. I take it with the spider
plant, outside. "Can't you make your doors wider,
love?" they gag. "Not here!" . . . the next house grows

everything wider, love included. There my books
will bud their meanings, saucepans bear fruit,
my boots, escaped, will climb a broader route.
"Here is the agent's photo. See how it looks

more spacious in every way. What do you think?"
"We'll manage. D'you want those dead flowers in the sink?"

## WHEREON

A hangover, too many cigarettes,
unanswered mail - soap thaws behind the taps,
the freezer's ribbed with polar ice. Who lets
the mice play hookey on the idle traps?
I do. I lead a life of small regrets.

The dog's duvet is thatched with grit and hair.
Wash it? No! Turn the slightly cleaner side
like my new leaf, resolved to stand and stare;
this shambles is perfection modified.
I find my flawed Utopia everywhere.

## THE ROVERS ARMS

I'm pestered, goaded, tortured, racked:
it's August and the pub is packed
with journey-making, tedious bores
who must traipse off to foreign shores
to bring back tans and lurid snaps,
with anecdotes. One day perhaps
when I have had enough to drink
I'll tell them what I really think.

I abominate your tales,
I cannot stomach the details
of what you ate, and where you went,
and who you met and what you spent.
I loathe, reject, detest and spurn
that way you show off your sunburn
and yap with smug complacency.
You are anathema to me.

Why should I empathise or care?
It seems to me that once you're there
you like to feel yourself at home.
Why take the trouble, time, to roam
to seek some little bar or dive
that replicates this one that I've
lurked in all summer? Don't you fmd
that travelling narrows the mind?

# FACE THE WEEK

Losses drip on the mat in envelopes,
wastage and endings trickle from the phone,
the floor's awash with spilt milk - all your own,
it's Monday morning, gutter of small hopes.

Drizzle, bad news, fresh bloodlettings of bills:
where is the tourniquet, how can you stop
your red life leaking out? Look, there's a drop!
Quick! Gulp down the placebo and the pills.

The days will tick on coffee cups and fags,
tomorrow may be better, the week-end
ahead holds open cheques for you to spend,
the working week's a dog but its tail wags.

## RECALL

A draft c.v. - its chapter titles bold -
where is the narrative, the unmarked tide?
The named is, from that date of birth, as old
as happenings, Tippexed, yet multiplied.

Present address: a decent terminus,
but I have lived in freer air than this.
Marital status: I suppose that's us,
laying down payments on a mortgaged kiss.

Exams and education: I can't tell
what tutoring brought consciousness about.
Strengths? Weaknesses? My carapace, my shell
hardened around a soft self loose with doubt.

Shred the pro forma - I will start again,
with birth pains, inkblots, smells and wasted time,
failures, too much to drink and other men,
jokes, friendship, dances, silliness . . . I'm

choked by the thickness of my loss. A sob
returns me to the present chance. Good job.

## GETTING THE MESSAGE

I've bought a B.T. answerphone,
it has a built-in voice,
in bossy yet mellifluous tone,
(and seeming to rejoice),
she gloats - it cuts me to the bone:
"You have no messages."

The emphasis is on the "NO",
the lady condescends
to speak (she stays incognito)
to one who has NO friends,
whose glowing digits always show:
"You have NO messages."

I cannot let that woman think
that I am on the shelf
NO life, NO lovers, on the brink -
I'll go and phone myself . . .
tonight the L.E.D. will blink:
"You have ONE message."

An invitation, party, fun,
oh! how she'll envy me!
Each day I'll add a different one,
and fill my diary,
next week she must admit I've won:
"You have SIX messages."

## ACUITY

Amongst old lies that wise men tell
is one that never hoodwinked me;
I know that flower, this stone, that tree
cannot endure beyond my spell.

When I withdraw they pass away,
my senses bring them all to life,
my eyes, hands, acting as midwife
at substantivity's birth day.

I hear you murmur "egotist,"
at which I ask you how you cope
with reality's tachistoscope,
should truant objects still exist.

The brain demands a decent shield
to save it from plurality,
from damage done to you and me
by superflux, if unconcealed.

Shut down most facets of the mind,
admit my solipsistic view:
perception is both clear and true
when the observer grows purblind.

POPPER[1]

Open the text at past laws: I,
deductive, will pop questions, try
old lags of theories with new tests.
Stand witness as I falsify.

Our love has died; at the inquest
I ask why heat was lost, suggest
your input failed and so I cooled
n the Ice Age since the arrest.

Heat's not reversible: that rule,
that entropy, quelled my last joule:
a chill cannot transfer, restore
pyrexia, even in a fool.

Absolute zero: the third law
will not admit so cold a score,
but, since we're there, the theory's blown,
no warmth is left to start a thaw.

Our system's closed; my quiz has shown
a universe now overthrown,
a Pheonix, killed when fully grown.
Love is not borrowed, nor on loan,
like scepticism, it is my own.

[1]*(Summarised briefly, the three laws of thermodynamics, developed in the nineteenth century, state that: heat input must be maintained to produce continuous energy; energy cannot be sustained by transferring heat from a cold body to a hot body; absolute zero of temperature is never reached. In the twentieth century Karl Popper argued that hypotheses are unprovable and can only hold until they are falsified.)*

## REVOLUTION[1]

Holography of language: moving words
exhibit meaning in reflected light,
the speaker's colours need the hearer's sight
to fly in format like migrating birds.
One beam of bright attention sets them free,
they wing, bring summer into frozen minds,
one swallow and the thirsting listener finds
the source of sense in glistening filigree -

an easy flight from brain to ear to brain.
Yet grand designs, 3-D, call for a laser,
coherence, new, projected, like a razor
cuts centuries of darkness. Who will stain

the future air with patterns read as blood,
write in the sky like Darwin, Marx or Freud
their sentences of death? We can't avoid
the execution of our favourite old falsehood.

[1] *(Some holograms produce images when ordinary light is reflected from them but others produce a 3-D image only when laser light is projected through them.)*

## IT'S ALL IN THE DAY'S WORK

Before surgery, Doctor Nash buys fruit:
palpates the pears, reads symptoms of decay.
The woman serves with hands like ginger root,
packs bleeding strawberries, cherries that may

contain defective cells within the bunch
jaundiced bananas, fevered redcurrants,
Coxes that fail when it comes to the crunch,
malingering melons, waiting like patients

who won't admit he can't relieve them all.
Some cases bruise and rot beneath the skin.
He finds notes, stethoscope, tells Miss Threlfall
he's ready now, and lets the first one in.

It's her, the shop-keeper. Her scan has shown
a tumour, size . . . let's see . . . of a grapefruit,
she senses it inside her like a stone,
covers her face with shaking ginger roots.

# HOMAGE

March 1st: out came the plastic daffodils -
they lasted through till June, to be replaced
by plastic roses. In Miss Pugh's cupboards
the seasons vegetated, washed, ignored
until their natural time unfurled; no waste
of fallen petals, spent, on windowsills.

I smiled until she died; but did not dare
to send a plastic wreath. Clean, greenhouse-grown,
same-sized chrysanthemums in cellophane
curled back from the reality of rain,
from handfuls of authentic soil now thrown
upon Miss Pugh, to show we truly care.

# BATHERS

Old women bobbing, three friends, hotel pool,
euphoric hippos in a watery playpen,
their kitchen heat of life has turned to 'Cool.'

Pre-puberty, aquadynamic eels,
they practised curving towards the world of men -
now widows flip a cleaner pair of heels,

acquire a shapeless body's innocence,
unwanted breasts, overstretched abdomens,
swim like slow frogs, wash off experience.

Their memories are rinsed from acts of shame:
sweat, milk, blood, contraception, semen,
secretions, functions, furtiveness; they claim

their right to be sterile, to care for none,
none but themselves, to float as sexless children.
Let chlorine bleach away the mess that's gone.

## KNITTER, FISHER, PHILOSOPHER, BAKER

She casts on sudden stitches from loose skeins,
catches an Arran sweater, Fair Isle top
with ciphered patterns, coded purls and plains,
needles of flickering bone that never stop.
This is her craft: this is the way she lifts

wool into cloth like fishes into nets.
He traps with weaving: plaice, bass, haddock, sole
that flounder deathward, hauls them, weighs them, frets
that some escape on margins of the shoal.
This is his line: this is the way he drifts

to snare the shining ones, like thoughts that swim
through mindwaves of the thinker's fluid brain:
some fall into his words; some flash at him
and fin away, outwit him yet again.
This is his trade: this is the way he sifts

ideas like a pastry-maker's flour.
She raises shortcrust, flaky, choux and puff:
her pies decoy our noses, ambush our
keen senses with concoctions light as fluff.
This is her task: this is the way she gifts

to us - as they all do - the endless round
of circling chores and interlocking shifts.
Let no-one break it. See: no striking rifts
divide the chain of ants upon the mound.

## UNDERGROUND

Tube, overcrowded with concerns:
that woman, there, who fights a frown,
she's knitting from loose ends of time,
she'd like the lines of life to rhyme,
her forties are a hand-me-down,
each decade costs more than she earns.

That Evening Standard hides a suit,
in which, concealed, there waits a man,
his destination's off the map,
he reaches, cannot grasp the strap,
his now is never: someone's plan
makes him, for ever, substitute.

That couple purchase love on hire,
instalments bleed their arteries dry,
their future will be interest-free,
his hand is ponderous on her knee,
she pats it as she guesses why
he is her owner-occupier.

It takes a child to know he's bored,
and pull the red, forbidden, cord.

## ON THE TRAIN

The accountant's lap-top grinds: its disc is etched
with digits representing numbers: he
reckons his life's perfection multiplied,
cash flows through spread-sheets screened creatively,
balanced by asset stripping. Close beside

him rests the sculptor whose keen hand has sketched
a lean portfolio of statuary
that he will rough-hew, chisel, chip and chase;
his slender figures beckon a stout fee,
the one thing he won't whittle down. The face

posed opposite, bones carved, eyes raked, skin stretched,
has launched wars from a thousand tall cat-walks,
models with heroin chic and razored cool
designer gear for bodies shaped to stalks
by anorexia - like the girl from school

who sits apart and watches. She has retched,
thrown back, all day, what she's been offered: food
to make her grow up, puff out - maths and art.
Her mind remains a skeleton, a nude,
one day she'll clothe it. Let the journey start,

take her, with them, to termini far-fetched
but all too real when the guidelines stop.
You know - as I do - which one of the three
she must become to topple towers. She'll swap
her everything for Helen's legacy.

## MATTER OF FACT

Let's deconstruct that word 'sincere'.
A child is born: its parents hide
a darkness happening inside;
they should feel joy - and do - but fear

strikes at the cradle of the mind.
Care they must; yet beyond care
casualty stalks the air.
Will accident or hazard find

a way into their softest place?
The victims of atrocity
on every newsreel that they see
come too close to their infant's face.

Now ask the mother with the pram,
foul weather covers, tiny head:
"Are you a hostage held by dread?"
Do any answer, "Yes, I am"?

## BUILDING MATERIALS

He's two and raising bridges out of wood
bricks that compose the structures in his head.
Can he remember towers from yesterday,
the pyramids and fortress of lost play,
bombed by the warning call of time for bed,
a daily siren, partly understood?

At four, his Lego farmstead lasts a week,
round plastic poppers keep his world in place,
men, goats, sheep, tractors on the kitchen floor
expand their territory behind the door
till Fairy Liquid hands reclaim their space
and clean away his tears with hide-and-seek.

School teachers provide other building blocks:
sums, reading, writing shape to maths and French;
his mind, like his packed lunch, is full and dry,
he does his homework where the byre and sty
were tolerated from the adult trench.
At last he gets results that no-one knocks.

At forty-two, an architect: he plans
a detached villa for his family
with peaceful room for all. He meets his team:
bricklayer, chippy, sparky; spills his scheme,
his wife assembles biscuits, cups of tea,
while he directs the distant artisans.

## FAMILY MATTERS

Between fateful, brief coitus and formation of the foetus
falls a super-power conflict of the genes,
when the colour of the eyes and the baby's nose's size
conduct sub-atomic battles. What that means

is that chromosomes dictate the results when parents mate:
one half of you is Dad; one half is Mum.
You were never in control - yours must be a passive role,
it's not your fault, whatever you become.

The procedure's complicated (as that sharp monk Mendel stated)
when more distant kin move in and do their worst:
DNA off Granny Mabel could ensure that junior's able
to do his sums. No? Grandpa got there first!

Human beings of all nations are the product of relations,
those ancestors that won the silent war.
Certain traits are dominant; if they're not the ones you want
you can't go back and change them at life's store.

Tootsies from Grandma Rita would be prettier and neater
than great-aunt's tendency to bunion, wart and corn.
It will be no laughing matter when you find you've got the latter -
small wonder that we cry when we are born.

## POLONIUS

"To thine own self be true." What fool
could give (or take) skin-deep advice?
The first layer's easy, cleanly, cool,
all sanitised. Don't dare to slice

to where that saw encounters mess:
a hundred selves avoid the tool,
pick one, examine it, confess
you won't wear that. The old man's rule

opens a gutsiness inside;
you would not wish your wife to guess
which secret organ chose the bride,
still cherishes her (more or less).

The surgeon's knife is too precise,
false closure is more dignified,
sincerity's too high a price,
the tumour's safe within your hide.

## MOVING ON

An English country scene, Miss Marplesland,
a village, ponded, manicured and treed.
What have the curtains netted? Underhand
the carving knife is double-edged in deed.

Windowlened glass, cars buffed and moss-free lawns.
the postman's bike and oh-so-British birds.
Who kills behind the clichés? No-one mourns
the victims of the sharpened stab of words.

Neighbourhood watch keeps the detective out.
Holmes cannot hear a dog that does not bark.
When walls are deaf the prisoner's last shout
is unattended by the copper's nark.

Soap opera? Melodrama overdone?
The medium is the message in our street.
The butler didn't do it just for fun -
we've closed that book. The ending's obsolete.

The genre's changed. There is no body now
but self-inflicted wounds bleed just the same.
Watson would find it elementary how
in New Britannia, no-one is to blame.

## PUBLICITY

Private. Beware the Dog. It rears
with eyes like blitz lights, extends claws,
probes with its microphonic ears,
masticates rumours in its jaws.

Give it a sop. Call: "Here, boy!" Pat
its muzzle, offer it a lead,
a sound bite. Will it stop at that?
If not, try bare flesh with its feed.

Too late, too near. Now you complain:
"This hell-hound is too wild to tame;
I meant the other kind of game."

It smells your furtive need for fame.

## FAMILY OUTING TO THE IMPERIAL WAR MUSEUM

We thought (she's seventeen months) she'd sleep throughout:
under a Zeppelin her eyelids fell,
stayed shut beneath the Spitfires, past the tanks,
Sherman, Mark V (they crushed men of all ranks
in mud). That gun fired the first British shell
in France, a thirteen-pounder. This dug-out

part of the Trench Re-creation (minus lice,
rats, casualties, rum, swearing) gives first hand
experience of what a Tommy felt.
His uniform's on show: boots, Mills bomb, belt,
his letters home, gas helmet - understand
one mite of what it meant to find the price.

And still she sleeps through Hitler's rise to power,
Munich, the phoney war, evacuees,
Dunkirk, blitzkrieg, munitions, ration books,
while I return to childhood. Memory looks
at posters and my generation sees
her great-grandparents struggle with their hour.

You, now (her mother and my daughter) hope
your little girl won't wake at Little Boy -
her nap lasts till the Secret War; she loves
machines, presses Enigma buttons, moves
the cogs, decodes signals, saves a convoy,
her female hands help the Home Front to cope.

Outside, she chases squirrels, hides, shouts, "Boo,"
beneath November skies of Air Force blue.

## NEW YEAR'S DAY: 1943

In childhood, on our chimney's back,
(as flames from bombed-out docks blazed higher)
two-headed Janus, sooty black,
guarding our tamed and rationed fire,
showed, at the turning of the year,
the face of hope, the face of fear.

Illicit chicken, traded lard,
dry carrot pudding - raisin-free
- whist and pontoon with dog-eared cards,
the triumph of utility,
when mothers fused, for girl and boy,
the face of hardship, face of joy.

"Mum, what are U-boats really for?
Can I go in that shop they've blitzed?
What's on the news when there's no war?"
I put my arms up to be kissed,
and Uncle Arthur glanced and smiled
at face of mother, face of child.

But then she wept and scolded me:
"You're old enough to have more nous . . .
Once we had clotted cream for tea . . .
It's only luck they've missed this house . . ."
I gazed into the hearth and saw
the face of peace, the face of war.

## S.O.S.

On shingle, funnelling out to sea,
I sat: around me new-hewn rocks,
by each, jetsam of shirts and socks,
and notices: "Mortgage, H.P.

commitments, self-assessment forms,
smart cards, year planners, mobile phones:
now pile them high on these gravestones
and take the plunge to be re-born."

Tube-loads of merchant bankers came,
shed Filofaxes and promotion,
ran boxer-shorted, to the ocean.
Oh! how they loved this latest game!

And superwomen, superslaves,
dived off glass ceilings, swooping free,
cast weights of earned equality,
and breast-stroked gently, making waves.

I envied but I did not throw
my ballast, lest I should capsize:
I flew the flag of compromise
crewed by the devils that I know.

## REVELATION

I bought a CD-Rom of hidden things,
the blurb was pink with promises: I read
of oystered mysteries revealed - misled
I mouse-clicked on a thousand coverings

and off they whisked. No Trade Description Act
could fault performance: I saw brains and hearts,
earth's core, dark moons, times gone, alchemic arts -
I snorkelled amongst cities of drowned facts.

Next day, I rang the helpline, pressed the star
button for queries, not complaints: "How may
I now re-cache my rainbow disc and play
with toys well wrapped, not knowing what they are?"

LEAP SECOND[1]

This night, an extra pip of time
is yours, is hers, is his - and mine:
one second of discrepancy
between the stars' chronology
and countdown of atomic clocks
throws double tick amidst the tocks.

What will you do with yours? I might
reach to my lover in the night
and, at a touch, confirm regrets,
resynchronise and cancel debts
of trust unpaid - then, with that leap
regain, at last, unguarded sleep.

Or should the superfluity,
that moment, gifted, hanging free,
be used to cast away a coin,
as practice, that I may rejoin
a lighter self and slower Earth?
The penny dropped has greatest worth.

Tomorrow's dawning will be late,
but let those men at Greenwich wait
a second until you and I
have had our extra mirth or sigh.
I'll send a bee to clocks of flowers,
if they must measure days and hours.

[1] *"Clocks around the world will stop for one leap second at midnight GMT. The Earth has been turning too slowly," said the director of the International Earth Rotation Service. (Daily Telegraph).*

THE CATCH

Low tide, half moon, dragnet: we four
and our kids, coached to break the law,
in silence, torches dimmed, minds full
of the illicit fish we'd pull
from icy, phosphorescent seas,
neck-deep (and drunk or else we'd freeze).
Draw in the haul of shimmering scales,
plaice, sewin, bass, as big as whales,
so we recall it, next day, when
in the grey-suited world again,
the magic's in the fridge on plates.
We beat the cops, the fish, the Fates.

That's long ago and childhood's flown,
the story (like the fish) has grown.
"How could you," some do-gooder says,
"teach children such immoral ways?"
But I know that they learned that night
some harmless wrong; some potent right:
respect for fishes' (and men's) skills,
the elements and natural thrills,
they found the strength to turn their back
on man-made ecstasy - and crack.
They watched their parents; now they know
that adults can be fools also.

## HEAVY METAL

Her ears are pierced with waiting holes;
gold sleepers stop them for a week.
What then? Her adolescent chic
will find new fleshpoints, novel goals

for studs, for skewered rings, man-traps:
three through her navel; next, her nose -
she breaks the piggy-bank and blows
the lot. Behind it, baby snaps

show her, bare, pudgy, on a rug,
unmarked except for dimples. Her
father reaches one down, asks: "Where
has she gone now?" Her mother shrugs.

ACTION REPLAY

A snap-shot, crumpled, fading, you and I,
twenty-somethings, careless, drunk perhaps,
both laughing - though three decades' casual lapse
has taken out the cause, the reason why.
The prudish lens refused to capture where
your straying, roving hands began to flirt;
a fade-out as I smoothed my too-tight skirt
and sudden passion scorched the waiting air.
What happened then, far back, develops now,
as printed somewhere on my filming mind:
me in the mirror, you erect behind,
suggestive, whispering: "Shall I show you how
I love you still?" We kiss, caress and laugh,
dissolve to faces from that photograph.

## DISTANCED

Are you surprised by violence?
The vandal's boot kickstarts a shock,
a rape assaults genteel pretence
that all is well behind the lock.

Yet seize your mind to separate
the vicious act from consequence,
the latent synapses of hate
electrify within the fence.

Suede fists, reluctant to catch blood,
pocket their anger as they wait,
a man-trap, hidden in the wood,
is - like a good slave - out of date.

We're guarded by the moving clock,
the hangman's put away his hood,
the serial killer stalks your block -
would you erase her if you could?

## DEFAMILIARISATION

Four shades of grey can map a hackneyed world;
the paintbox, padlocked with a routine key,
needs a Houdini colour to burst free,
splash brilliance to four corners, foxed and curled.
A child,

a child sees through the loophole - look with him:
raindrops hose dazzling oceans round his feet,
his Wellingtons, red dinghies, sail the street -
throw off your commonplaces, let them swim.
Love,

of course, new love, will freshen, quicken, make
all things, once jaded, novel, green and spruce,
the life you've worn threadbare with excess use
can be recovered. Let sleeping wolves awake.
A fever

and its strange aftermath can disconnect
you from the outside robots wheeling past:
commuter, postman, vet, builder, typecast
drift through a fading gauze. Let us neglect
the glass,

the dusty window with its measured view
and press our foreheads to a loosened pane,
let minds escape the frame, the old mundane
familiar, that toad. I'll fly with you.

## BERLIN WALL[1]

'The fox knows many things; the hedgehog knows
but one large thing.' Through history they scour:
meaning is prey. Shakespeare, foxy, devours
his scattered themes from taverns, thrones, hedgerows.

A centrifugal mind, a sweeping brush
seeks out, rakes up morsels so far diverse:
a fleeing boy, a Moor, a garrulous nurse,
flowers, swords, an anti-social dog. A blush

that symbolises boldness and yet shame -
these are the pickings of the scavenging fox,
a blow-out with no menu. His meat shocks
the thinker with no stomach for rich game.

The hedgehog's brain feeds only on its likes:
consistent slugs that nourish his design,
coherent, unitary, anodyne,
fanatical, well guarded by his spikes.

[1]*Isaiah Berlin's 'The Hedgehog and the Fox' uses the quotation from the Greek poet Archilochus to divide human minds into two different types.*